Original title:
The Whimsy of Woodlands

Copyright © 2025 Creative Arts Management OÜ
All rights reserved.

Author: Alec Donovan
ISBN HARDBACK: 978-1-80567-395-8
ISBN PAPERBACK: 978-1-80567-694-2

Whispers in the Leafy Canopy

Squirrels chatter, plotting pranks,
Mice are giggling by the banks.
Rabbits dance in dappled light,
While owls wink with all their might.

In this realm of leafy fun,
Where every shadow loves to run.
The trees are laughing, swaying high,
As butterflies flit and sigh.

Dappled Dreams Beneath the Boughs

Mushrooms wear their polka dots,
While chipmunks jive in silly spots.
The sunlight flickers, plays a trick,
As dandelions sway and flick.

Beneath the boughs, a toad sings loud,
In tune with critters, spry and proud.
Laughter bounces through the glade,
As dreams and smiles are freely laid.

Secrets of the Sylvan Realm

Leaves exchange their gossip sweet,
While squirrels play hide-and-seek fleet.
The brook chuckles, smooth and clear,
As frogs crack jokes from yonder sphere.

Grasshoppers jump to bold new heights,
While lazy bees have dance-off fights.
The whispers tickle, twirl, and tease,
In this realm of playful ease.

A Dance of Dandelions and Pines

Dandelions wear crowns of gold,
With secrets of laughter yet untold.
Pines sway gently in the breeze,
Mimicking giggles from the trees.

A butterfly twirls in its flight,
Chasing shadows in pure delight.
With every bounce, the world feels new,
As joy rolls in with the morning dew.

Riddles on the Riverbank

A frog wears glasses, quite absurd,
He reads the news in a chirping herd.
The fish all giggle, splash, and dive,
While turtles tease him, oh so alive.

The riverbank holds secrets and cheer,
As otters dance with no shred of fear.
A crab gives wink, and the herons sigh,
In this curious place, time drifts by.

The Hidden Heartbeat of the Forest

The trees have gossip, branches sway,
  Whispers tickle the leaves all day.
  A squirrel chuckles at a fallen nut,
  While shadows play in a funny rut.

Beneath the ferns, a dozy fox yawns,
Dreaming of days spent munching on fronds.
  The heartbeat echoes, a playful tease,
As bunnies jiggle with the buzzing bees.

Laughter on the Leafy Lanes

Down the leafy lanes, laughter's found,
Where shadows hop and giggles abound.
A ladybug spins in delightful haste,
While a beetle scoffs, claiming it's a race.

The daisies chuckle as they bloom wide,
While butterflies flutter, full of pride.
Each step is a dance, a merry charade,
In this lively lane, worries cascade.

Whirling Through the Wildflowers

Through wildflowers, a tumblebee flies,
With comical spins and buzzing sighs.
A butterfly winks, sharing a joke,
As daisies dance in a floral cloak.

The poppies nod, their heads in glee,
While gnats make mischief, so carefree.
With petals and laughter swirling about,
Nature's punchline, we all shout!

Secrets of the Soaring Canopy

In the tops where squirrels play,
They trade their acorns all day.
One wears a hat that's way too grand,
And dances around on a high branch stand.

A parrot drops a joke on the breeze,
As tree frogs practice their silly tease.
The leaves giggle when the raccoons chat,
Each story wrapped in a funny spat.

Fireflies wink in a darting race,
As shadows fall with a playful grace.
The owls hoot, quite out of tune,
While the sun dips low like a bright balloon.

Beneath the Boughs

Under the boughs where the shadows loom,
A rabbit bakes pies in a mushroom room.
A fox in a cloak tries to dance and sway,
But trips on a log, and it's a real display.

The butterflies wear tiny shoes,
As the beetles play tag, shouting wild news.
A hedgehog provides them a berry treat,
While squirrels serve tea on whimsical seats.

There's laughter among the flowers bright,
As the sunset paints the sky with light.
Each critter sings their favorite song,
In a woodland party, you can't go wrong.

Elves Amidst the Evergreens

Elves with hats that wobble and twirl,
Craft tiny toys with a giggly whirl.
One slips and falls into a sap trap,
While his friends all chuckle and sing a clap.

They play hide and seek within the trees,
While bees buzz happily, aiming to please.
A mischievous pixie throws a small dart,
And the laughter echoes, a woodland art.

Mossy carpets for their little feet,
As knots of laughter make each day sweet.
With sprigs of thyme, they weave their cheer,
Creating a laughter that all can hear.

Treetop Tea Parties

In the treetops, tea parties thrive,
With acorn cups and the best high-five.
The owls wear glasses, so very wise,
While raccoons giggle with cake on their thighs.

The wind brings tales from afar,
Of a fern that once wished to be a star.
The daisies dance in delight and glee,
As butterflies spin about, wild and free.

Every sip is a secret surprise,
With shimmer and sparkle in their eyes.
Beneath the sun, the fun goes on,
With laughter that lingers, from dusk to dawn.

Mischief Among the Mossy Stones

Beneath the stones, the frogs do dance,
In rubber boots, they prance and prance.
A thistle poke gives a funny yelp,
As squirrels giggle, feeling quite kelp.

A snail wore shades, looking quite cool,
While crickets played on a toadstool pool.
Hares raced past in a jolly spree,
As beetles laughed: "You can't catch me!".

The ants had a parade, all in a line,
They marched with banners, feeling divine.
A caterpillar joined the fun, oh my,
Did a cartwheel right before July!

In mossy beds, they tell tall tales,
Of flying fish and other gales.
With every laugh, the woods take flight,
Inviting all to join their delight!

Curiosities of the Canopy

Up in the trees, the owls wear hats,
And gossip loudly, chatting like chaps.
A raccoon chef, with a spatula grand,
Serves berry pancakes, on leafy land.

A squirrel quiz master, making a fuss,
As birds compete, without any fuss.
The prizes? Nuts, and shiny things,
Resplendent joy that the forest brings.

With swinging vines, the monkeys perform,
In acts so wild, they break the norm.
And butterflies flutter, like confetti blooms,
Adding flair to this circus of rooms.

Up high they laugh, beneath the moon,
In a jolly ruckus, a merry tune.
Each branch a stage, each leaf a review,
Where nature's jesters find laughter anew!

Revelry in the Rustling Leaves

Amidst the leaves, a party unfurls,
With spinning spiders and dancing pearls.
A chipmunk DJ spins records loud,
While mushrooms bop, joining the crowd.

The wind whispers jokes, tickling the trees,
As laughter echoes through rustling leaves.
A hedgehog winks from his cozy nook,
And reads from the forest's own funny book.

Twigs join for drinks, a tea made of dew,
With honeysuckle sweet, and a dash of blue.
A broomstick ride, for the brave few,
Who dare the flight, in a sky so true.

Under a glow of twinkling stars,
They celebrate life, forgetting their scars.
In every giggle, a world so alive,
Where nature's magic allows them to thrive!

Serenity of the Sun-dappled Path

Sunlight giggles on the winding track,
As shadows dance with a smooth backdrop.
Mushrooms pop up, wearing skirts of lace,
While giggling grasshoppers win the race.

A wise old owl surveys the show,
With a twinkle in his eye, a glimmering glow.
He sways along, with quite the charm,
While rabbits hop away, raising alarm.

A tortoise sips tea, so slow and grand,
With dandelions served, oh isn't he planned?
And bugs in tuxedos, polished with care,
Attempt the tango in the warm, fresh air.

This path invites giggles, whispers, and cheer,
Where nature's all-folk gather near.
Every rock, every leaf, tells a tale so bright,
Of the humor found in the soft morning light!

Mysteries Beneath the Moss

Beneath the green, a secret sleeps,
A tiny gnome counts all his sheep.
With acorn hats and laughter bright,
They frolic under a toadstool light.

A squirrel spies and starts to grin,
As hedgehogs join the goofy spin.
They slip and slide on mushroom caps,
Sharing giggles in silly laps.

Old trees snicker at the show,
Their roots wiggling, ready to go.
As owls hoot in the midnight air,
The moon just laughs, with silver hair.

What secrets lie in shadows deep?
Is that a rabbit with a leap?
Join the fun, come take a look,
In the mossy pages of a storybook.

The Laughing Leaves

In autumn's breeze, the leaves take flight,
They swirl and twirl in sheer delight.
A leaf named Larry does a spin,
Saying, "Catch me! Come on, let's begin!"

With every gust, they dance and shout,
Making faces, what a rout!
They play peekaboo on branches high,
As clouds drift lazily in the sky.

With colors bright and laughter loud,
They tickle branches, feeling proud.
A game of tag, oh what a scene,
In a tapestry of gold and green.

So if you hear a rustling cheer,
It's leaves at play, so don't you fear.
Join the fun, just take a glance,
And maybe you'll get caught in their dance.

Tales of Twisting Trails

On winding paths where secrets bloom,
A crooked stick whispers 'gloom'.
Yet, nearby, a fox with a wink,
Says, "Don't fret, just have a drink!"

A foolish frog leaps in surprise,
While dragonflies wear glittery ties.
They tell tales of spots unseen,
In the shimmering woods of vibrant green.

A wobbly bear in fuzzy socks,
Loses a race to playful rocks.
Cheering stones, they hum a tune,
As bursts of laughter fill the noon.

So follow the giggles, let them lead,
On twisted trails where dreams proceed.
Adventure waits in every thrum,
With playful whispers, come have fun.

Dreaming in Green Shadows

In shades of moss, the fairies scheme,
Baking cookies with a giggly beam.
They sprinkle joy with every stir,
As crickets join in, a tiny blur.

A dreaming bear snoozes by a brook,
With goofy dreams in every nook.
What will he dream? A giant pie!
With dancing ants that laugh and fly.

In the shadows, a rabbit's plot,
To take a nap in a sunny spot.
But oh, what tricks the flowers play,
They giggle, hiding him away!

So wander deep in nature's fold,
Where giggles echo and tales are told.
In every leaf and every glance,
There's whimsy waiting—take a chance.

The Trail of Twinkling Stars

In the night, the fireflies dance,
Bouncing round in a merry trance.
Whispers of laughter fill the air,
As trees giggle without a care.

One owl hoots a silly rhyme,
As crickets strum in perfect time.
The moon joins in, a glowing clown,
Wearing a smile, never a frown.

Acorns tumble, a wild parade,
Squirrels giggle, the mischief made.
A raccoon winks, his mask in place,
In this glimmering, starry space.

Oh what fun beneath the sky!
Where all the woodland critters lie.
With twinkling stars above them glowed,
They dance and play, their joy bestowed.

Wonders of the Winding Woods

In paths where shadows stretch and bend,
The trees seem to chat, their branches send.
A fox wears boots—so bright, so fine,
While rabbits sip from cups of brine.

Mushrooms gossip underfoot,
Saying, "Let's dance, not just sit!"
While the brook laughs with a bubbly song,
The trees nod along, oh it's so wrong!

Up ahead, a grumpy old bear,
Begins a jig without a care.
The squirrels clap with acorn chimes,
As nature bursts in joyous rhymes.

In this place where tickles roam,
Every creature finds a home.
A merry dance in leafy nooks,
Where magic lives in storybooks.

Enigmatic Echoes

Echoes of giggles bounce from trees,
As a hedgehog rolls like a tumbleweed breeze.
A wise old owl plays peek-a-boo,
While shadows sass in the twilight hue.

Branches wiggle, a dance they crave,
While beetles moonwalk, so bold and brave.
A chorus of chuckles fills the night,
As fireflies twinkle, a whimsical sight.

The fox wears sunglasses, such a show,
Strutting like he's got nowhere to go.
All the critters join in the spree,
Their laughter weaving through every tree.

In echoes of whimsy, all unite,
Creating mischief till morning light.
With nature's giggles and chirps of glee,
The forest of fun is forever free.

Harmonies of the Hummingbirds

Hummingbirds buzz in vibrant suits,
Playing jazzy tunes to their roots.
Bumblebees join with a buzzing cheer,
While flowers sway, dancing near.

Wings twirl like cotton candy dreams,
As frogs croak out hilarious themes.
A butterfly flutters just for fun,
Flashing colors, oh what a run!

The breeze chuckles as it passes by,
Tickling leaves with a gentle sigh.
Each creature sings in harmonic play,
Their symphony brightens the day.

In this haven, where laughter thrives,
Magic flutters, and joy arrives.
As melodies blend in lighthearted flight,
The woodland's charm is pure delight.

Fables Woven in Willow's Embrace

In the shade where shadows dance,
Squirrels spin their tales of chance.
A rabbit dons a tiny hat,
While hedgehogs juggle just for chat.

The willow whispers secrets low,
As dancing mushrooms start to glow.
A spider weaves a silly rhyme,
Tickling leaves with laughter's chime.

Frogs debate beneath the stars,
Arguing who has the best guitars.
With lightning bugs as audience bright,
They croak their songs into the night.

But once the dawn begins to rise,
The woodland critters close their eyes.
And in the hush, all still and calm,
They dream of mishaps sweet as balm.

Moonlit Murmurs Among the Ferns

Underneath the silvery moon,
Crickets play a silly tune.
A raccoon dons a mask of glee,
While badgers laugh, oh what a spree!

The ferns sway with a gentle jig,
As dancing fireflies start to dig.
With tiny spoons, they feast on dreams,
And drink the dew in funny streams.

Owls hoot softly, wise and quaint,
While wolves pretend to be a saint.
In this wood, with friends so dear,
Laughter floats like night-time beer.

As dawn's first light peeks through the trees,
They scurry home with webs of tease.
And in the break of day so mild,
The woodland continues as a child.

The Brush of Mossy Fingers

Mossy fingers tickle ground,
Playing games without a sound.
A snail races with a laugh,
While ants take turns to share the path.

The mushrooms giggle, tops held high,
As tiny specks of spores drift by.
Each puff is met with wild delight,
A cloud of laughter in flight.

Beneath the branches, soft and cool,
Raccoons gather for a duel.
Decked in leaves, they pose for show,
While woodland critters shout, "Go, go!"

But when the twilight starts to rise,
The mischief turns to sleepy sighs.
And as the stars twinkle above,
They drift to dreams of silly love.

Portraits in the Glistening Gloom

Deep in the glistening shade they pose,
In frames of leaves where laughter grows.
A fox in glasses strikes a tune,
While bees buzz softly, sweet as June.

Silly mice paint with berry hues,
Creating scenes of woodland views.
A deer's dramatic flair takes flight,
As crickets croon a Broadway night.

The moonlight twirls through clover beds,
Where dreamers dance on nature's threads.
Each step a splatter, bright and bold,
In this gallery of stories told.

But as the night grows thick and warm,
These portraits smile, a jesting charm.
In the watery glow of silver beams,
Their laughter lingers, weaving dreams.

Twilight Treetops

In twilight's glow, the branches sway,
A raccoon wears a hat, what a play!
Owls hoot a tune, out of tune,
As fireflies dance in the silver moon.

Squirrels trade nuts like kids on a spree,
With acorn bling, oh so fancy!
Branches creak with laughter anew,
While shadows blend in a comical hue.

A Serenade for the Squirrels

Squirrels gather, a band in the trees,
Barking out rhythms, with grace and ease.
Nutty notes float, quite out of key,
As chirpy birds join in with glee.

They strut and dance on slender limbs,
A wobbly jig, their humor brimmed.
Furry performers in nature's hall,
With acorn props, they have a ball!

Frolics in Ferns

In lush green ferns, where mischief hides,
A hedgehog rolls with squeaks and glides.
Frogs leap in sync with a splashy cheer,
While mice play tag, their giggles near.

Beneath the leaves, a rabbit scoffs,
He cheekily nibbles, 'Oh, watch me, folks!'
With twirls and leaps, they chase the sun,
Nature's comedy, oh what fun!

Butterflies and Brambles

Butterflies flutter in colorful flings,
As brambles giggle, tangled strings.
Bees buzz in circles, a fuzzy ballet,
While ladybugs cheer in red and gray.

In this woodland show, no frowns do peek,
Each critter plays, a unique tweak.
With playful jabs and a wink so bright,
They weave a tale, a comical sight!

Mischief Among the Mushrooms

In a cap of red, a bug did dance,
With little yellow shoes, he took a chance.
A squirrel watched on with a cheeky grin,
Whispering tales of the fun to begin.

Toadstools giggle with every small breeze,
Flipping their skirts, aiming to tease.
A mouse with a hat, he joins the fun,
Chasing shadows till the day is done.

Frogs croak a tune from the pond near by,
While butterflies flit in a whirl and fly.
With every step, the laughter spreads,
As woodland creatures play games in their beds.

So join the frolic, let spirits rise,
In a world of mischief, under bright skies.
For here in this realm, joy is the key,
Where mushrooms and friends delight and agree.

Fluttering Fables in the Ferns

A rabbit tells tales to a friend, a fox,
Of enchanted dreams and old wizard's clocks.
A hare in a vest starts to sing a song,
While ferns nod along, where they all belong.

The wind takes a turn, tickles a tree,
That sways and whispers, 'Come dance with me!'
Squirrels tumble down in a cartwheel spree,
While wise old owls hoot, 'Let it be free!'

A hedgehog recites, with a flair for drama,
About the lid of a teapot named Grandma.
With giggles and glee, the stories take flight,
Beneath leafy shelters, into the night.

In the midst of fables, our laughter blends,
Creating a magic that never ends.
So come gather 'round, as the sun gently sets,
In a land of delight, with no regrets.

Tales from the Treetops of Fantasy.

Up high in the branches, where kangaroos leap,
A parrot confesses, 'I'm not here to sleep!'
From trunk to twig, the stories unfold,
Of daring young mice and their treasures of gold.

A badger in boots leads a conga line,
While squirrels shout, 'Hey, it's party time!'
Acorns are flying, like confetti in air,
As creatures of all stripes dance without care.

A tree stump declares itself king of the woods,
With a crown of green leaves and mossy hoods.
Everyone cheers, 'Long live the tree!'
In a realm of oddities, joyous and free.

So climb up with glee, to the tops of the trees,
Where tales spin like webs in a whimsical breeze.
In each little nook, find laughter anew,
As fantasy thrives in bright woodland hue.

Enchanted Glades

In the glade where the daisies wear crowns of delight,
A dancing beetle twirls, feeling oh so bright.
With a thump and a thud, the young otter slides,
As merry as can be, where the laughter abides.

A fox in a tutu, prancing around,
Makes friends with a cricket that leaps off the ground.
They gather the flowers and weave them with care,
Creating a garland, a whimsical flair.

As shadows grow long, the stars come to play,
An orchestra forming, in a magical way.
With fireflies twinkling, like jewels in the night,
The glade sparkles softly, a jubilant sight.

So wander the paths where the joy knows no end,
In magical realms, with nature's own blend.
For laughs and sweet mischief are always entwined,
In the heart of the woods, where love you will find.

The Magic of Maple Mornings

Beneath the maple's leafy crown,
Squirrels wear hats and dance around.
A raccoon plays a tiny flute,
While ants in booties shake their roots.

Morning dew like crystals shine,
Bouncing bubbles, oh so fine.
A fox with goggles rides a snail,
Tails wagging in a silly trail.

Birds gossip over breakfast fare,
Chirping tales beyond compare.
A hedgehog juggles hazelnuts,
As laughter flows from furry guts.

So grab a seat and join the jest,
In nature's circus, we're all guests.
Maple mornings full of cheer,
Where every critter brings a smirk near.

Winding Paths in Wonderland

Down the trails where mushrooms sway,
Trolls juggle mushrooms all the day.
Fairies zoom on bumblebees,
Sharing gossip with the trees.

A snake in goggles slithers by,
While bunnies hop and play the sly.
A worm in shades, so dapper, sits,
Crooning ballads that make us splits.

Every twist and turn we take,
Brings laughter, oh, make no mistake!
A hedgehog winks, and silly signs
Point us to the land of pines.

So follow paths where giggles dwell,
With every step, hear nature's spell.
In this amusing woodland spree,
Nothing's ever quite as it seems.

Songs of the Swirling Stream

By the stream, the water sings,
While frogs wear crowns and flappin' wings.
The fish throw parties, splash and leap,
As crickets hum their tunes so deep.

With oars made of twigs, they row in glee,
A turtle plays the tambourine, you see!
The rocks join in, they tap and twirl,
As bubbles rise and dance, oh, what a whirl!

In the shallows where ripples prance,
Dragonflies lead a silly dance.
The breeze brings notes of laughter bright,
As sunlight sparkles, pure delight.

So gather 'round the babbling bliss,
Where nature's chorus can't be missed.
Join in the fun, sing along,
As waves of joy create our song.

Sunlit Silhouettes

When the sun begins to rise,
Shadows stretch in funny guise.
A rabbit's shadow wears a hat,
While dancing squirrels spin and chat.

The trees throw arms, all twisted high,
Tickling clouds drifting by.
A bear pretends to sip some tea,
Wearing shades, so carefree and free.

In the light, the forest beams,
Whiskers twitch with silly dreams.
Leaves clap hands, the scene's a breeze,
Nature laughs, oh, how it pleases!

So take a stroll, enjoy the view,
Where sunlight makes the world anew.
With every glance, giggles are met,
In silhouettes that won't forget.

Whirlwinds of Petals and Pine Needles

In a rush of petals, they swirl and spin,
Squirrels dance wildly, to a tune on the wind.
Sunbeams peek through, with a giggle and cheer,
While chipmunks play tag, without any fear.

A dandelion sneeze, sends seeds up to soar,
While mushrooms gossip of tales from folklore.
A deer with a hat made of comical leaves,
Cautiously tiptoes, while giggling grieves.

The bumblebees buzz in a muddled delight,
As frogs wear their crowns, and croak out goodnight.
With owls in their glasses, giving wise little winks,
It's a party of nature, who knows what it thinks!

So come join the frolic, where laughter's the key,
In a world of whimsy, oh come, take a peek!
Where each step you take, holds a giggle, a squeal,
And woodlands come alive in a most funny reel.

Sylvan Secrets Beneath Emerald Canopies

Under the green, where secrets reside,
Rabbits throw parties and squirrels collide.
With ivy-clad gnomes sharing sly little jokes,
The trees bend with laughter, what playful old folks!

A raccoon in pigtails steals berries for fun,
While shadows twist about, as if on a run.
The wind tells of tales that make creatures laugh,
As ants wear tiny hats, heading to a craft.

With fireflies twinkling like stars in a game,
The woodland world whispers, "who's winning the fame?"
Beneath emerald canopies, jokes intertwine,
Even the mushrooms join in, feeling quite fine!

So tiptoe through laughter, beneath leafy skies,
Where each rustle and chuckle brings joy that complies.
For here in the forest, where laughter's the rule,
Every critter's a jester, in nature's grand school.

The Sway of Wildflowers and Whispers

Wildflowers sway with a whimsical grin,
As gossiping breezes spread tales from within.
A ladybug giggles, saying, "Oh, what a day!"
While butterflies twirl, in a fanciful way.

Dancing in circles, the daisies all chatter,
While hedgehogs in ballet shoes make a great clatter.
The sunflowers plot with the bees in a scheme,
To turn the whole meadow into a grand dream.

An owl's on a swing, with a dance of delight,
As the crickets join in, playing tunes throughout night.
A thistle in teacups, wearing a crown,
Chuckles out loud, as he tumbles down.

And so in the clearing, where laughter takes flight,
The whispers of wildflowers glitter with light.
In each flutter and giggle, the magic's alive,
In the sway of the blossoms, oh how we thrive!

A Tapestry of Twilights and Twists

As twilight creeps in, the mischief begins,
With shadows that waltz, and the laughter that spins.
The moon wears a smile, while stars give a wink,
And crickets recite poetry, faster than you think.

A fox in a cape, dodges twigs with a leap,
While owls plan a heist for the best fruits to keep.
The mossy old rocks hold secrets galore,
As hedgehogs assemble behind the big door.

Every twist holds a chuckle, every turn brings a grin,
As raccoons in pajamas prepare for a win.
The fireflies gather, like lights on a tree,
Turning night into magic, wild and free.

In the heart of the woods, with laughter to fit,
In tapestries woven from the whimsy of wit,
So dance with the shadows, let joy take its place,
For nightfall's a canvas, a whimsical space!

Whirlwind Across the Woodland

A squirrel spun tales of acorn gold,
While birds tweet secrets, daring and bold.
The leaves join in, with a giggling sway,
As breezes whirl through, in a playful ballet.

Mushrooms donn hats, all colorful and neat,
Dancing on roots to a rhythm so sweet.
The rabbits start hopping, with jittery grace,
Making a ruckus in this leafy place.

Chipmunks do flips, with a wink and a cheer,
While shadows of trees have a secretive sneer.
A whirlwind of jest in the soft, green grass,
Where laughter is loud and the days hurry past.

Flickering Firefly Dreams

Fireflies twinkle like stars on the ground,
In a jiggle and flash, they twist all around.
They light up the night with a giggling glow,
Creating a canvas where dreams freely flow.

A frog in a tux, with a croaky refrain,
Leaps from a lily, again and again.
The crickets are tap-dancing, just for the show,
Encouraging fireflies to steal the night's glow.

A buzz of delight through the whispers of air,
Each flicker a secret, a playful affair.
And as dreams come alive in this magical dome,
Even the moon seems to call this place home.

The Enigma of the Emerald Canopy

A riddle unfolds in the shade of the trees,
Where whispers of wind tease the rustling leaves.
A parrot demands the attention of all,
With jokes so absurd, they make even time stall.

The owls wear glasses, enigma and guile,
Pondering riddles that stretch for a mile.
While woodland gnomes in their knitted green hats,
Giggle at mushrooms that think they're like cats.

With branches that wiggle, all dressed in delight,
The canopy chuckles, embracing the night.
And every odd creature joins in on the fun,
As shadows play tag 'neath the sparkling sun.

Fables of the Fern-filled Folly

In a patch of green where the ferns shout with glee,
A tale spins of critters, as quirky as can be.
A hedgehog in boots sauntered under the sun,
Claiming the path till the day's merry done.

There's a snail with a story that stretches for years,
And a family of ants that perform with no fears.
With arms made of twigs, they put on a play,
While the foxes cheer loud, "Hip hip hooray!"

The fables weave laughter through each leafy glen,
Where every odd creature is welcome as kin.
In this fern-filled folly, all hearts feel the spark,
And joy blooms anew with each laugh in the park.

Silhouettes in the Sunlight

In the glen where shadows dance,
A squirrel wears a funny pants.
With acorns stored, he takes a leap,
While giggling frogs begin to peep.

Beneath a branch, a rabbit spins,
Doing cartwheels, cheeky grins.
A sunny day, a playful chase,
Round the tree, they slow their race.

A snail with shades went for a stroll,
He stops to chat with a playful mole.
They swap tall tales of grand design,
And knock-knock jokes that intertwine.

As sunlight fades and laughter swells,
The woodland whispers, joyous spells.
They bid goodnight with giggles bright,
In dreams, they dance 'til dawn's first light.

Mirth Beneath the Maple

Beneath the branches, funny things,
A woodpecker in coal, he sings.
Dressed in outfits far too loud,
He hops around, a wannabe crowd.

The chipmunks hold a dance-off grand,
Chewing nuts, they form a band.
With rhythm wild and moves so spry,
They jig with leaves, oh me, oh my!

A raccoon pranks, all in good fun,
Disguised as chef with spoons to run.
He stirs the pot of honey sweet,
And serves it on his furry feet.

The sunset glows; it's time to play,
In echoes of laughter, night holds sway.
With tickles from the softest breeze,
They share their joy among the trees.

Burrows of Bliss

In nooks and crannies, secrets dwell,
Where creatures gather, tales to tell.
A hedgehog dons a woolly hat,
While rabbits joke, 'What do you think of that?'

Fluffy tails tickle the ground,
As giggles dance and jump around.
Their burrow's filled with bright confetti,
As they cast spells with laughter, ready!

The owls convene with wise old eyes,
Discussing art—an acorn prize.
They toast with berries, make a clink,
'Your turn to shine! Come, don't you think?'

Beneath this earth, a merry hub,
With whispers soft, they share the rub.
As night draws near, they dream in cheer,
In rambunctious burrows, joy is near.

Reverie in the Rustled Reeds

By the pond where dragonflies roam,
A frog sits poised, calls it home.
With tiny crowns and royal hops,
He hosts a party—never stops!

The reeds sway gently, a dance routine,
With whispers soft, they share the scene.
A party crab puffs up with flair,
While muskrats munch without a care.

The turtles roll in laughter's tour,
As they ponder jokes—simple, pure.
With splashes loud, they call the ducks,
Who waddle in with quacking plucks.

As stars peek out, silly and bright,
The woodland creatures end the night.
With whimsy wrapped in cozy dreams,
They laugh and play beneath moonbeams.

Wandering Souls and Wistful Trees

In hats of moss, the trees do sigh,
As squirrels engage in a acorn pie.
A raccoon juggles, oh what a sight,
While owls debate, who's wrong or right.

Beneath their limbs, shadows play,
With breezes whispering, 'Come out and stay!'
The sun peeks in, with a cheeky grin,
While flocks of birds dance, hoping to win.

A frog in a vest hops with flair,
While rabbits do yoga without a care.
Old roots chuckle, sharing old tales,
Of all the mischief that never fails.

With laughter ringing, a merry tune,
Where flowers bloom and giggles balloon.
In every nook, a tale unfurls,
Of funny frolics in leafy swirls.

Luminous Layers of Leaf and Light

Sunbeams tickle the leaves awake,
While chipmunks play, for fun's own sake.
Butterflies don their finest attire,
In this goofy fest, they never tire.

A breeze lifts hats from furry heads,
As the wise old turtle chuckles in spreads.
With every rustle and schtick and squawk,
The woodland begins to giggle and talk.

In a spotlight grin of shimmering hue,
A jolly raccoon bids its friends adieu.
As shadows waltz on the forest floor,
The bugs in tuxedos prepare for more.

Stars peek out with a laugh and a wink,
As nighttime arrives, creatures rethink.
Under the moon, the mischief ignites,
In layers of laughter, the joy ignites.

Quirks of the Quaking Aspen

Aspens shake in a giggly line,
As whispers tell of squirrels divine.
With cheeks full of cheeks, acorns in store,
The trees erupt in laughter and more.

In swirls of white, they prance and sway,
With crickets chirping their own ballet.
A bear in a tutu takes center stage,
As all woodland critters act their age.

Chasing their tails, the dogs run amok,
While beavers tap dance, making their clock.
Oh, the quirks that these aspen expose,
With every rustle, another tale grows.

Under the stars, their giggles ring,
In the heart of the night, the creatures spring.
Funny and free, they twist and shout,
In a forest of fun, there's never a doubt.

Hidden Havens in the Hush

Such secrets lie where shadows dwell,
In hidden nooks, they weave their spell.
A playful fox with a jingle bell,
Consults with owls on wonders to tell.

A shy hedgehog spins tales of woe,
While laughter bubbles from below.
The trees lean closer to hear each prank,
As chuckles swim through a winding bank.

A badger acclaims, "I'm the king of night!"
While fireflies twinkle, a dazzling sight.
Slumbering flowers giggle and bloom,
In the hidden havens where whispers zoom.

With the hush of dusk comes giggly chats,
Where laughter grows like blooming sprats.
In every corner, joy's out of view,
These hidden havens know just what to do.

Caressing the Canopied Calm

A squirrel wears a tiny hat,
Chasing shadows, like a spat.
Leaves begin to giggle, too,
As laughter echoes, sweet and new.

A snail rides on a beetle's back,
Plotting mischief, making a hack.
Branches sway in playful cheer,
Whispers of secrets, soft and clear.

A raccoon dances, quite a sight,
Beneath the stars, so warm and bright.
With acorn drums, he sets the beat,
The woodland band's so hard to beat!

A robin jests with little wings,
Telling tales of silly things.
Breezes join the merry jest,
In this space, we're truly blessed.

The Heralds of Harmony

A parrot's squawk sounds like a tune,
While frogs croak loudly, night to noon.
The ivy smiles, a cheeky grin,
Among the vines, the fun begins.

Bumbling bees in a funny race,
Chasing butterflies with grace.
A fox in boots, flamboyant trick,
Carts around the trees so quick.

Chirping crickets join the song,
Singing to the night so long.
Twinkly stars slip in the fun,
While owls hoot, "You've just begun!"

A raccoon juggles with delight,
While fireflies flicker, oh so bright.
Nature's laughter fills the air,
In a world that's wonderfully rare.

A Tapestry of Treetops

A tapestry spun from leaves of green,
With colors bright and sights unseen.
Branches twist in a festive fight,
Creating shadows in the light.

A chipmunk wears a dapper coat,
Balancing acorns on a boat.
With laughter ringing, echoing free,
In the concert of the old oak tree.

Wandering spirits, sweetly they prance,
With little feet in a woodland dance.
Dancing with daisies under the sun,
Creating marvelous, silly fun.

A toad sings opera, all out of tune,
While mushrooms nod beneath the moon.
In this gallery of aged bark,
Every tale leaves a charming mark.

Fanciful Footprints in the Forest

In the forest, footprints play,
Leading us on a merry way.
A bunny hops, its ears a-flop,
Guiding dreams, we can't stop.

Misty paths and giggling trees,
Whisper secrets in the breeze.
A hedgehog rolls in fallen leaves,
A theater of joy, the heart believes.

A deer, adorned with flowers bright,
Stands, surveying the silly sight.
With every chuckle that we share,
The woodland spins, beyond compare.

Footprints fade like morning dew,
Yet memories linger, sweet and true.
In this realm of laughter and play,
Joy unfolds with each new day.

Enchanted Paths Where Fairies Dwell

On mushroom stools, they sit and grin,
With twinkling eyes, mischief to begin.
Scattered sparkles sparkle in the air,
As giggles bounce from here to there.

They dance with leaves, a merry sight,
Crows wear hats, oh, what a fright!
Squirrels act as cheerful jesters,
While rabbits play, and foxes fester.

Toadstools play the bongo tunes,
While fireflies flicker under moons.
A garden gnome, so out of place,
Lost in thought, with a silly face.

So wander through this joyous land,
Where silly creatures take a stand.
In every nook, a laugh awaits,
Embrace the fun, and leave your fates.

Sylphs in Sundappled Glades

In shades of green with laughter bright,
They spin and twirl, a joyful sight.
With petals soft as pillows lie,
As butterflies prepare to fly.

The brook hums tunes, a silly song,
The trees nod lightly, joining along.
A fox, adorned with daisy chains,
Winks at all, as mischief reigns.

The dappled sun starts to play peek,
As giggling pixies chase a streak.
With acorn cups, they sip their tea,
And share tales of their wild glee.

So wander where the laughter sows,
In shimmering fields where wild thyme grows.
With whimsical friends, you'll find delight,
In this forest of sheer nonsense, bright.

Lullabies of the Forest Floor

A fox croons low, a silly tune,
Underneath the watchful moon.
Crickets chirp their rhythmic dance,
While sleepy frogs leap in a prance.

Mossy carpets, soft as dreams,
Hide tiny sprites, or so it seems.
With giggles muffled, held so near,
Each shadow whispers what you hear.

The raccoons raid a picnic spread,
With donuts rolling, they'll be fed.
And as the owls hoot through the night,
A prime-time show with pure delight.

So lay your head on leafy beds,
And dream of giggles, as fun spreads.
For every rustle, every snore,
Is just the lullaby of the forest floor.

Echoes of the Enchanted Grove

In the grove where echoes chat,
A squirrel plans a secret spat.
With acorns aimed and giggles loud,
He joins his friends, a silly crowd.

The owls debate, who hoots the best,
While hedgehogs play the game of jest.
With shadows flitting to and fro,
The whispers of secrets begin to flow.

A dance party of bumblebees,
Twirl 'round trees in their buzzing spree.
The playful mist swirls with a tease,
As nature laughs in joyful ease.

So follow sounds of joyful cheer,
In echoing paths both far and near.
For in this grove, quite whimsically,
Every moment's marked with jubilee.

Shadows in the Thicket

In the thicket where shadows dance,
Squirrels prance in a nutty trance.
Frogs in tuxedos, quite a sight,
Croak their songs through the quiet night.

Bunnies hop with a twitchy nose,
Wearing hats made of leaf and prose.
A fox takes bets on who can run,
While owls chuckle at the fun.

Crickets play tunes on old tree logs,
As wise old trees gossip with frogs.
They trade tall tales of the past,
While fireflies blink — oh, what a blast!

So if you wander where laughter dwells,
Join the woodland of quirky spells.
With your friends, happy and tight,
In the thicket, the shadows ignite.

The Playful Pines

Among the pines, a game unfolds,
Where playful whispers tickle and scold.
The needles giggle and sway with glee,
Rustling secrets, a grand jubilee.

Trees don glasses, a sight to behold,
Narrating stories, both silly and bold.
The wind dances, a mischievous sprite,
As squirrels trade jokes under moonlight.

A raccoon juggles acorns with flair,
While woodpeckers chirp without a care.
They cheer him on with raucous applause,
In the playful pines, they break all laws.

So join the fun where laughter thrives,
In the heart of pines, where joy arrives.
A whimsical world, both bright and fine,
Forever spinning in a piney line.

Gentle Giggles of the Grove

In the grove, where laughter reigns,
The flowers speak in silly refrains.
Bees wear bonnets, oh, what a sight,
Buzzing along, they bring delight.

The daisies dance, twirling so sweet,
While mushrooms tap to their own beat.
Ladybugs play hide and seek,
Giggling softly, oh so meek.

Trees toss confetti from their great height,
As the sun paints everything bright.
Breezes join in with a soft sigh,
Echoing giggles that seem to fly.

So wander here, where joy is sown,
In the grove, feel never alone.
With gentle giggles and a smile,
Stay for a while, let laughter compile.

Darting in the Dappled Light

In the light where dapples play,
Critters dart in a merry way.
Chipmunks race in their striped coats,
While caterpillars float like boats.

Breezes tickle the grass all day,
As rabbits hop and make their way.
Each step bursts funny little sounds,
In the joyous dance of the ground.

The sparrows chirp with comedic flair,
Trading jokes in the open air.
With every flutter, giggles spread,
Creating cheer where laughter's bred.

So come, dear friend, to this bright space,
Where dappled light brings smiles in grace.
In this wonderscape, joy ignites,
Darting here, within delightful sights.

Secrets of the Sylvan Realm

In the woods, a squirrel steals
Acorns tucked with crafty zeal.
The mushrooms giggle, round and stout,
As fearless rabbits leap about.

A fox in specs reads poetry,
While grasshoppers hop with glee.
Trees gossip in the cool, soft breeze,
A parade of ants, buzzing with tease.

Beneath the boughs, a frog sings loud,
To guests of flowers, all adorned and proud.
A ticklish vine wraps round a stone,
Whispering secrets all its own.

In moonlit nights, the fireflies dance,
Their tiny lights a flickering chance.
With every laugh, the brook joins in,
A quirky world where giggles begin.

Echoes of the Evergreen

Beneath the pines, the shadows prance,
A raccoon's mask invites a glance.
The toadstools, in a silly row,
Mimic jigs with all their glow.

A sneaky badger with a grin,
Hides in bushes thick as skin.
Whispering winds, they chuckle and poke,
As the owls hoot a witty joke.

The trees around pretend to sway,
In rhythm with the fox's play.
Barking spiders weave their thread,
With giggling beetles rising ahead.

In every nook, mischief fills the air,
Squirrels trip and tumble unaware.
Lost in laughter, the brook joins fast,
Echoing joy that's sure to last.

Whispers Among the Trees

A jolly woodpecker knocks a beat,
While chipmunks shuffle on little feet.
The branches shake, a playful jest,
As owls eavesdrop, enjoying the rest.

Among the leaves, the shadows play,
Creating scenes that tease and sway.
A gnome in a hat, with a wiggle of toes,
Winks at the flowers, secrecy grows.

Mice in cloaks throw parties grand,
With cheese and jam, all carefully planned.
The thickets stir with twinkling light,
As nature giggles in sheer delight.

At dusk, a dance of frogs unfolds,
As fireflies tell stories untold.
Laughter rolls under the starlit dome,
In this quirky kingdom we all call home.

Dance of the Dappled Sun

Sunbeams twist through leaves so green,
Creating patterns, bright and keen.
A playful breeze swirls leaves around,
In every rustle, joy is found.

Squirrels dart, their tails a blur,
Chasing shadows that dance like they stir.
Butterflies giggle while sipping dew,
While flowers gossip, old and new.

The brook runs by with a splash and a grin,
Teasing the rocks where tadpoles swim.
The sun dips low, painting the sky,
As nature winks, letting worries fly.

With each sunset, the woods come alive,
Whispers of laughter in every dive.
In this merry realm of light and fun,
Joy blooms sweetly under the sun.

Rhapsody of Rustling Leaves

Leaves giggle as they twirl,
Squirrels dance in a playful whirl.
With acorns tossed in cheerful glee,
They chuckle in their leafy spree.

A rabbit hops, a bear takes a chance,
In this grand forest, all join the dance.
Pine cones roll like bowling balls,
Nature's jest in its curious calls.

The wind whispers jokes to the moss,
While each tree laughs, never a loss.
The sun peeks through, wearing a grin,
As critters chuckle; let fun begin!

So here's to the trees and their leafy song,
Where laughter and joy just can't go wrong.
In this woodland theater, fun's on display,
Come join the merriment, come out and play!

Traces of Tiny Footsteps

Tiny paws tapping on the ground,
A trail of chaos can always be found.
Little creatures in a scampering race,
Chasing their shadows in a funny chase.

A mushroom peeks from its leafy nook,
Wonders what mischief those critters took.
The grass waves high as they dash about,
An acorn's flip brings laughter out.

Squeaky shoes on a deer's wild run,
Each step a story, each step is fun.
Caught in mischief, a mole's little plot,
Ends with a giggle, a ticklish spot.

The forest echoes with tiny grins,
As each little critter scrambles and spins.
In this madcap dance of zestful retreats,
The steps of the tiny are joyful feats.

Sunbeams and Shadows: A Woodland Tale

Sunbeams poke through branches wide,
In shadows, a hedgehog tries to hide.
But giggles burst from behind a tree,
As sunlit spots claim the day with glee.

A crafty fox plays peek-a-boo,
With butterflies swirling in skies so blue.
When shadows tease, the laughter grows,
In this woodland wonder, sly joy flows.

A squirrel stashes nuts with flair,
Wearing his stash like a fancy hair.
Each beam of light a cheeky jest,
As cozy critters find prankish rest.

Oh, this tale unfolds in bright delight,
With every flicker, and shadowy bite.
Dance with the beams, laugh with the shade,
In this forest story, fun's never delayed!

Treetop Serenades at Dusk

Birds chatter tales from their lofty place,
While croaking frogs join in the race.
Branches sway as the moon's glow beams,
A chorus of laughter drifts in dreams.

The owls hoot jokes, both wise and bright,
While fireflies twinkle, gleeful in flight.
Each flutter a wink, each blink a play,
In this twilight choir, night steals the day.

Raccoons tiptoe with masks of surprise,
As playful racquets hide in their eyes.
A one-legged hop from the cheeky crow,
Sets off the giggles in evening's glow.

So listen closely as dusk unfolds,
For secrets of laughter in shadows it holds.
Treetops sing tunes of fun and delight,
In this merry symphony of night.

Hues of Harmony in Nature's Palette

Leafy greens dance in sunlight's glow,
Mushrooms wear hats, putting on a show.
Squirrels debate, which nut's the best,
While clovers giggle, feeling quite blessed.

Bumblebees buzz with a goofy charm,
Spreading sweet news without any alarm.
A rainbow of colors, a feast for the eyes,
Nature's own circus beneath the blue skies.

Hopping rabbits, with shoes on their feet,
Waltz through the forest, keeping the beat.
Each flower's a dancer, spinning with glee,
This playful parade is a sight to see.

So come join the fun, leave worries behind,
In this crazy realm, laughter you'll find.
With each silly creature and whimsical sight,
Nature's own humor shines ever so bright.

The Liveliness of Larks and Lichens

Up in the trees, a lark sings its tune,
While lichens chuckle, just past noon.
Foxes with glasses read stories aloud,
As mushrooms applaud, forming a crowd.

A rabbit on stilts hops over a log,
Chasing a dragonfly, misty as fog.
The grass plays coy, tickling feet in delight,
As dancing dandelions sway through the night.

Owls wear monocles, wise and discreet,
Debate who's the best with a cheeky tweet.
The breeze carries whispers, jokes shared between,
Every leaf joins in, a comedic scene.

With laughter erupting from branches and brush,
It's a wild party, come join in the rush.
Each creature a character in nature's grand play,
Bringing fun and mischief to brighten the day.

Gossamer Threads of Forest Folklore

In twilight's glow, where shadows abide,
A spider spins tales with its silk thread wide.
Mice in tuxedos attend a grand ball,
While crickets recite, standing proud and tall.

Shiny acorns roll, plotting their quest,
While a wise old crow leaves them to quest.
Fairies on swings laugh in the air,
Making wishes with whimsy, without a care.

The wind whispers secrets, delightfully weird,
As pinecones play poker, all happily cheered.
A deer with a bow tie shakes hands with a frog,
Two best friends, lost in their chat by the bog.

So gather 'round, let your imaginations soar,
In this delightful place with laughs to explore.
The tales of the forest are funny and bright,
Where wonder dances freely, under moonlight.

Breezes of Bewilderment and Bliss

Gentle breezes tease the grass beneath,
Causing squirrels to giggle and breathe.
Branches creak laughter, old stories retold,
As hedgehogs wear capes, nature's knights bold.

Dandelion seeds float, a balloon parade,
While frogs in their bowler hats serenade.
Clouds join the fun, with shapes that combine,
A dog, a cat, all in sunshine's design.

The brook babbles gossip, cheeky and spry,
While beetles debate if they can fly high.
Each rustling leaf holds a punchline so fine,
In this bustling world, humor's divine.

So laugh with the ferns, let your heart sing,
Join the woodland revelry, let the joy spring.
With every delight, in the air it will play,
Blissful bewilderment is here to stay.

Squirrelly Soiree

In the trees, they flip and twirl,
A furry crew with tails that swirl.
Pinecone hats and acorn shoes,
Racing round in nutty hues.

They chatter loud, a lively sound,
As giggles echo all around.
With seed confetti in the air,
It's a dance, without a care!

From branch to branch, they leap and dive,
Jumps so wild, they barely survive.
A scrumptious feast of berries bright,
Ending with a pie-fueled flight!

As moonlight casts its gentle glow,
The wildest party starts to slow.
With sleepy yawns, they drift away,
Tomorrow brings another play!

Glistening Paths and Glowing Nights

Mushrooms glow like lanterns fair,
Bouncing shadows everywhere.
Frogs in tuxedos leap and croak,
Underneath the starry cloak.

Crickets serenade the night,
With chirpy tunes, a pure delight.
A wandering deer in silk and lace,
Trips on roots, what a funny face!

Raccoons wear masks, just like thieves,
Stealing snacks from autumn leaves.
The owls hoot in comic glee,
As squirrels giggle from a tree.

When dawn breaks through the leafy shade,
Messy antics must be paid.
With hangover feels of playful blight,
They'll rest until the next wild night!

Forest Frolics

Bouncing bunnies race for fun,
Playing tag under the sun.
Chipmunks drum on hollow logs,
While painting spots on lazy dogs.

The hedgehogs roll in grassy fields,
Dressing up in floral shields.
Madcap runs and tumbles, too,
In this place where laughter's true!

Tall trees sway in gentle breeze,
Wobbling like a merry tease.
The flowers giggle, tickled bright,
Dancing round from left to right.

At day's end, they gather near,
For tales of joy, they give a cheer.
But one last sprint, just for the day,
Chasing clouds, they slip away!

Cartwheels Through the Canopy

Kooky critters flip and spin,
Worms in tutus join the din.
With cartwheels crafted on a whim,
The squirrels giggle, fortunes brim.

Lively lizards twirl in glee,
Swinging wide from chubby trees.
Each leaf a stage for acrobat,
The whispers swirl, the chatter chat.

With every roll, a comic fall,
As bumbles bounce, they hear the call.
Through dripping branches, they unite,
In laughter's grasp, they take to flight.

Soon the stars start blinking down,
As night wraps round the playful town.
Tomorrow's tricks await in store,
For woodland friends and tales galore!

Fauna's Fancy

In a clearing where squirrels play,
They dance and leap, in a silly sway.
A raccoon winks, wearing a hat,
While birds gossip, chattering like that.

A hedgehog rolls on a log, quite proud,
Singing tunes a tad too loud.
Beneath the leaves, the critters peek,
Finding joy in the games they seek.

Butterflies paint the air with glee,
Tickling noses, as sweet as can be.
A chipmunk juggles acorns with flair,
While the rabbits cheer from their grassy lair.

Through the trees, laughter echoes bright,
Nature's circus, a true delight.
Each creature wears a comical grin,
In this merry wood, where fun begins.

Lost in Lilac and Leaf

In a lilac haze, a deer forgets,
Where it left its shoes and pets.
It prances around, in pure dismay,
While butterflies flutter, leading the way.

A wise old owl, perched on high,
Watches the antics with a knowing eye.
With a wink and a hoot, he shows the way,
To the lost fawns who just want to play.

Beneath the ferns, a snake plays tricks,
Turning into a knot, just for kicks.
Laughter erupts from nearby trees,
As critters join in with giggly wheezes.

The sunset brings a challenge anew,
To find the way home, who knew?
But with chuckles and jests, they roam,
In this magical place, they call home.

Secrets of the Sunlit Spell

In the glare of sunbeams, shadows shift,
Mice in capes with magic gifts.
They cast silly spells, a sprinkle and pop,
Turning flowers into candy drops.

A toad with glasses reads the map,
Leading the gang to a whimsical trap.
A giggling brook plays tricks on the shore,
With splashes of water, who could ask for more?

Frogs make crowns from the finest lilac,
Whilst the bees buzz in a raucous track.
Every tree whispers secrets with glee,
As nature's whimsy holds the key.

When night falls, the stars will dance,
Fireflies join in a twinkling trance.
Though magic fades with the darkened sky,
Tomorrow will come, and laughter will fly.

Breezy Whispers of the Birch

Under birches where the breezes tease,
A raccoon dances with the flickering leaves.
With a wiggle and jig, he steals the show,
As acorns tumble, and giggles flow.

A family of foxes plays peek-a-boo,
Ducking and dodging, just for you.
With puffy tails and bright, sly eyes,
They weave through the grass, just like the skies.

The whispers of wind carry jokes untold,
As a squirrel recounts tales of old.
Blowing lighthearted tunes through the trees,
Nature hums along, with gentle ease.

As twilight falls, a bonfire ignites,
The woodland critters share their delights.
With snacks of nuts and laughter a-burst,
In this merry place, fun always comes first.

Whimsical Wanderings in the Underbrush

In the thicket, mushrooms dance,
A squirrel in pants takes a chance,
With acorn hats on pompous heads,
They plot their world while avoiding dread.

A hedgehog juggles berries bright,
Chasing fireflies, what a sight!
The branches chuckle, leaves burst out,
While rabbits hop and sing about.

Over puddles, frogs start a band,
Croaking tunes, they make a stand,
The ants in choir, all tap their toes,
As laughter through the greenery flows.

In this forest, every turn,
Holds a secret, a chance to learn,
With creatures wise and mischief grand,
Together they wander, hand in hand.

Nectar and Nonsense Under the Stars

Under twinkling, cheeky skies,
The bees wear shades and make amends,
With flowers chuckling, sipping sweet,
A party's brewing, can't be beat!

A hedgehog plays games with a gopher,
While a tortoise proves he's a looper,
The fireflies join in the fun,
Illuminating like stars on the run.

The moon spills silver, laughter flows,
As crickets compete in funny prose,
Each blossom giggles with delight,
In petals bright, they dance all night.

With nectar spills and silly tales,
Even the owls join in the gales,
Hooting like jesters, full of glee,
In this charming nook, so carefree.

Harmony of the Hidden Hollow

In the hollow of trees so wide,
A band of critters take a ride,
With a mouse on drums and a cat on flute,
They make a scene, oh what a hoot!

The grasshoppers leap, creating beats,
While ladybugs dance on tiny feet,
The trees sway gently, hum along,
With whispers woven into song.

Bunnies giggle, tails in a twist,
While the wise old owl shakes his fist,
'Provide some order!' he does shout,
But the forest knows, it's fun, no doubt.

In this quirky realm, nothing's brief,
Laughter reigns as the main belief,
Where harmony blooms, it's plain to see,
That joy in the wild is the key to be.

The Language of the Lichen

On ancient trees, the lichen speaks,
In riddles wrapped with rainbow peaks,
With whispers soft, it shares its lore,
Of all the fun found on the forest floor.

A dancing snail with a sparkly shell,
Tells tales of mischief, oh so swell,
While moss joins in, with its green delight,
Creating echoes through the night.

A squirrel gestures, foolish and high,
Pointing to friendships with the sky,
As clouds giggle and gently swoon,
In this airy realm, beneath the moon.

So listen close to the stories shared,
In the heart of the woods, you'll be spared,
From worry and troubles, just take a chance,
In this playful realm, join the dance.

Echoing Laughter of the Elders

In circles of bark, the stories unfold,
The wise old trees chuckle, their secrets told.
They whisper of squirrels and hats made of leaves,
While raccoons dance jigs, the humor never grieves.

With roots that twist, they wiggle and shake,
The forest floor vibrates; what fun they make!
Their laughter continues, fanning the breeze,
As birds join the chorus, flitting with ease.

A gnome smirks beneath a mushroom so bright,
He overheard stories that tickled all night.
The flowers they giggle, their petals all sway,
In this tangled retreat where they've come out to play.

When shadows grow long, and the stars make their peek,
The old trees just shuffle, still playing their cheek.
Echoes of laughter ring clear as the day,
In a woodland realm where the merry hold sway.

Crooked Quotes from Creaky Trees

A maple declared, 'I'm sap-sucking sweet,'
While a pine moaned softly, 'My branches are beat!'
The oaks lent their wisdom, though crooked their glee,
'Embrace every knot, it's the way to be free!'

Whispered the willows, with bends that are grand,
'Life's too short to stand straight, just take a grand stand!'
While birches laughed loudly, 'We peel with such flair,
Those who can't handle us, don't bother to care!'

A timid old cedar chimed in with a grin,
'Sometimes you must wiggle the worries within.'
As laughter like raindrops fell soft on the ground,
The rhetoric twisted, but joyboxed around.

So gather your quotes, whatever they are,
From the echoing woods, they shine like a star.
Each tree has a tale, a chuckle, a sigh,
Sharing crooked wisdom that soars to the sky.

Joyous Journeys in the Greenery

In leafy canopies, the critters parade,
With each step they take, laughter's serenade.
A fox with a hat, mapping mischief in air,
While slugs in their shells are quite unaware.

The rabbits are racing, with hiccups of cheer,
While porcupines giggle, no worries or fear.
'Chase me!' cries one, with a leap and a twist,
Laughter erupts, it's a well-known tryst.

Twirling and spinning, the dance never ends,
As mushrooms join in with their fungal friends.
With twinkling eyes, they hop in delight,
In this sprawling playground, the sun shines so bright.

So wander the paths where the trail's never straight,
In the rich green embrace, let joy celebrate.
Each moment's a treasure, so silly, so spry,
In this verdant wonder where laughter runs high.

Laughter Amidst the Lilies

On lily pads dancing, the frogs hold a ball,
With a croak and a leap, they invite one and all.
Their jokes float like bubbles, so high and so round,
While the fish in the pond giggle up from the ground.

A turtle, quite nimble, tells tales of his race,
Saying, 'Slow and steady wins fun in this place!'
With ripples of laughter that shimmer and shine,
The reeds sway to rhythms, feeling just fine.

The dragonflies dart, with a shimmer and zing,
'They're throwing a party; come dance, it's a fling!'
While petals all blush, wearing smiles made of dew,
In this watery haven, where joy bids adieu.

So sink in the mirth where the lilies reside,
With each splash of laughter, let worries subside.
In the heart of the blossoms, with each gentle sway,
Find whimsy that tickles and brightens your day.

The Frolic of the Forest Folk

In the glen, the rabbits dance,
Wearing hats at quite a trance.
Saplings join in, bending low,
As the giggling breezes blow.

Squirrels twirl on branches high,
Chasing shadows that flit by.
With acorn hats and leafy capes,
They play jokes on passing drapes.

The wise owl cracks a silly grin,
As the hedgehog rolls on in.
With every tumble, laughter swells,
Echoed through the leafy bells.

Together they sing, so bold and bright,
A chorus of joy in the fading light.
In every nook, they find delight,
In giddy games till the stars ignite.

Overgrown Adventures

A fern tickles a wandering toe,
While mushrooms wear a dandy show.
A bear in boots struts down the lane,
Bouncing with rhythm, never in vain.

The slugs slide past in a comical race,
While a tortoise wears a smiley face.
Snails spin tales of sticky grace,
In their slow-motion, silly place.

A beetle dons a tiny cape,
As the hedgehog tries to escape.
With every twist, the forest's game,
Turns absurd and never the same.

Through dappled paths, they trot and play,
In a whirlwind of fun on a sunny day.
Each leaf and twig, a prop in sight,
For a frolic that feels just right!

Swaying with the Seasons

Spring's pranks bring flowers that giggle wide,
While bees pull faces, they cannot hide.
Sunshine tickles every petal's face,
As froggy friends sing with joyful grace.

Summer sways with dragonflies,
That wear sunglasses, oh my, oh my!
Grasshoppers leap with silly flair,
Joking with clouds, they float in air.

When autumn arrives, the leaves take flight,
Dancing in colors, what a sight!
Crispy crunches beneath each foot,
As squirrels play hide and seek in pursuit.

Winter brings snow with a soft, cold kiss,
While the rabbits hide, curled up in bliss.
Yet here in the chill, laughter stays warm,
In the heart of the forest, a cozy charm.

Magic in the Moonlit Meadow

Under the moon, the daisies cheer,
As fireflies buzz, drawing near.
The butterflies wear gowns of night,
Twinkling softly, oh what a sight!

A raccoon steals a fancy snack,
With a nibble here and a playful smack.
While the owls hoot rhymes so sweet,
Echoed in the rhythm of pinprick feet.

The hedgehogs glide on dew-strewn grass,
In a game of tag, oh what a laugh!
Each leap and roll, a cycle of fun,
Under the watch of a glowing sun.

With every twirl, the meadow gleams,
In a world woven from giggling dreams.
Magic whispers through every blade,
A symphony of silliness serenade.

www.ingramcontent.com/pod-product-compliance
Lightning Source LLC
Chambersburg PA
CBHW051658160426
43209CB00004B/945